# JEAN VANIER

## We need one another

### RESPONDING TO GOD'S CALL TO LIVE TOGETHER

spck

Original edition published as
*We Need Each Other: Responding to God's Call to Live Together*
by Paraclete Press, Brewster, Massacuhesetts, USA, 2018

First published in Great Britain in 2018

Society for Promoting Christian Knowledge
36 Causton Street
London SW1P 4ST
www.spck.org.uk

All quotations from Holy Scripture are the author's own translations and paraphrases.

*British Library Cataloguing-in-Publication Data*
A catalogue record for this book is available from the British Library

ISBN 978–0–281–08152–3
eBook ISBN 978–0–281–08153–0

1 3 5 7 9 10 8 6 4 2

Printed in Great Britain by Jellyfish Print Solutions

eBook by Fakenham Prepress Solutions, Fakenham, Norfolk NR21 8NN

Produced on paper from sustainable forests

# Contents

# *Preface*

I was happy in April of 2008 to visit the wonderful community of Saint Martin in Nyahururu, a small town in the central part of Kenya. That year was a memorable one in Kenya as it opened with violence and bloodshed in literally all parts of the country, particularly in the territory, major towns, and villages of the Great Rift Valley. In the wake of that violence, pain, and loss it was a gift to be able to gather together people from diverse cultural and religious backgrounds for a retreat, to listen and to reflect on the word of God. This book comprises the talks I gave during that retreat.

At my home, in the community of L'Arche in France, I have lived for fifty-three years with people with disabilities. They have revealed to me the face of God, his compassion and exquisite tenderness and love for each one of us. Those with disabilities have been my teachers and have gradually opened me to know and accept my own fears and disabilities. Their friendship has opened my heart to love and to growth. Their love has led me deeper into the loving heart of Jesus. The original community has now grown throughout the world. It is always the same message—people being transformed by people who are fragile. There are now 140 communities around the world with eighteen in the United States.

Around the world these communities offer hope to those who are marginalized in our competitive societies where few win, many lose, and more are victims. In 1967, together with Marie-Helene Matthieu we founded communities of Faith and Light, small groups of friendship, support, and celebration for people with disabilities, their families, and friends. These groups offer hope and transform lives, affirming the importance of each human being.

The title of this book—*We Need One Another: Responding to God's Call to Live Together*—is a reflection on the invitation of Jesus, who is asking us to become a friend of the poor and to befriend those we reject because of their color, their poverty, or their disability. This is not easy unless we go through a process of transformation that occurs as we listen to the message of Jesus. This message is that each one of us is precious to Jesus, whatever our culture, language, background, faith, ability, or disability. If we open our hearts to him, if we hear and respond to the cry of the needy, and if we enter in relationship with them and ask one another for forgiveness, we are gradually transformed.

Even though this book was originally a retreat given in Kenya, the words and message are essentially the truth of the Gospel, which is for people in all circumstances. Today we are living in a very stressed world. There is a lot of fear and even hatred for those who are different. Jesus came to preach peace and to break down the barriers that separate people. May this little book help each one of us become messengers of peace, of mercy, and of forgiveness.

*Jean Vanier*
*Trosly-Breuil, France*

# CHAPTER 1

# *What Are You Looking For?*

The next day John was there again with two of his disciples.

When he saw Jesus passing by he said, "Look, the Lamb of God!"

When the two disciples heard him say this, they followed Jesus.

Turning round, Jesus saw them following and asked, "What are you looking for?"

They said, "Rabbi, where are you staying?"

"Come," he replied, "and you will see."

So they went and saw where he was staying, and spent that day with him.

It was about the tenth hour.

(FROM JOHN 1)

Before coming to Kenya I was invited to a secondary school in Paris, and the students asked me why I was going to Kenya during such a turbulent time in the country. Could it become a dangerous experience?

I replied that I was going to Kenya to visit the community of Saint Martin, because I was convinced that I could find Jesus there. For me, faith is not enough! I need to touch, I need to feel, and I need to see Jesus in the life of the people. That is why I am going to visit the community of Saint Martin, because I am convinced that there I can touch, feel, and see Jesus. If you tell me that there is another community where I can meet Jesus—in China or any other place very far—I will go there because faith has never been enough for me.

I am happy to be with you here in Nyahururu. We come together at a moment when many have been deeply affected in recent days and months by violence in this and surrounding regions. We come together from many different places and cultures, bringing with us different histories, customs, and languages. We give thanks for the gift of being able to gather in peace and safety to reflect, share, pray, and celebrate together.

Each of us has a beautiful culture, and our mother tongue is the language that we receive from our culture. In my case, for many decades I've lived with people, many of whom do not speak with words. They speak with their bodies, they speak with their tears, and they speak with their smiles. It is important to understand these other languages, as well, that we all share. What are you saying? What are you living? Where is your pain? Where are your dreams? The reality of the world is that although we cannot always speak one another's language, we can still attempt to understand one another's pain, joys, hope, and dreams.

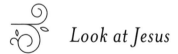 *Look at Jesus*

We read in the prologue of the Gospel of John that the Word became flesh to lead us into the knowledge of the Father, so that we can discover who God is. Right after the prologue, we hear of an incredible man, John the Baptist, who was sent by God to prepare the way, to help people to trust and to believe. John the Baptist is an extraordinary witness of God because he points to Jesus and says, "I am not important, he is important. I am nothing. I am not even worthy to undo the laces of his sandals. Look at Jesus." At one moment, John the Baptist sees Jesus from afar and he says to the people around, "Behold, look carefully, here is the Lamb of God who has come to take away all the hatred and violence and negativity that is in us." Jesus came to take away from our hearts all that is sin, our refusal of love and our closing ourselves up in fear.

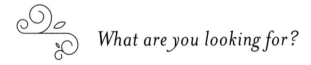

## What are you looking for?

The next day, John the Baptist is with a few of his disciples. Again, he sees Jesus and he says to his disciples, "Behold, look carefully, the Lamb of God." At that moment, two of his disciples break off from him and start to follow Jesus. One of these men is

Andrew and the other is probably John, who wrote the Gospel. Here we find Jesus walking and these two men start to follow him. Jesus turns around, and we hear his first words in the Gospel of John, "What are you looking for?"

This is beautiful. The first words of Jesus are not a command. He gently asks, "What are you looking for? What are your desires? What do you long for?"

I use these words of Jesus as a question to each one of you. Why are you here? What do you want and what are you looking for? It is very important to clarify what it is that you want, what your deepest desire is, and what you are looking for.

## Where do you live?

The two disciples were surprised that Jesus threw a question at them, so they simply asked, "Master, where do you live?" They had heard John the Baptist say that Jesus was the Lamb of God who would take away those fears that prevented them from welcoming people who were different. They realized that sin was the rejection of what was different and that hatred of the different could lead to warfare. These two disciples had also heard from John the Baptist that the man who stood in front of them was someone familiar with the ways of God and that he was somebody important. Then comes the question from these two disciples, "Where do you live?"

They are telling Jesus, "I want to spend time with you; I want to listen to you and possibly to be transformed by you. I want to escape the powers of egoism and selfishness that hold me to myself and prevent me from opening up, that prevent me from listening and from being in relationships with people who are different." Jesus questions the two men, "What are you looking for?" And they answer, "Master, where do you live?" to which Jesus simply says, "Come and see." So the disciples go, they see, and they spend time with him.

They stayed with him that day and they saw. What touches me is that this Gospel was written sometime around the year 90 CE. It was announced many times and finally it came to be written. I like to think of the old John, now maybe over ninety years old, saying: "I remember the first time I met Jesus . . . I was a disciple of John the Baptist. One day John the Baptist pointed at him and announced that he was the Lamb of God who had come to take away the powers of negativity and evil within me. So I followed him."

## *Have you met Jesus?*

I ask you the same question, the first question Jesus asked: Why have you come here and what are you looking for? When was the first time you had an experience of Jesus, that you really met him? I am not asking about the time you were baptized, but rather, about that moment when your heart opened, when you sensed that God loves you, and that you are important to him. When was that first moment?

Each one of us has a story. The story begins when our mothers conceive us after being in union with our fathers, and then as tiny little beings in the womb of our mothers we grow and finally experience that extraordinary moment of being born. It is not a moment we remember, but from the moment we are born, held by our mothers and then nourished from their breasts, we discover that we are loved. This is followed by moments of joy and of pain in the family and finally, at some point in our lives, there is a meeting with Jesus. Somehow a belief that Jesus is alive is born within us, a belief that he loves me and I am important to him. But this belief can become clouded when we are caught up in our different cultures and we forget about our meeting with him.

Our lives are filled with important moments. We have the moment of birth, the moments of childhood, and of sickness. Sometimes there are very painful moments when a parent or loved one dies, or when there are conflicts in the family. There are also moments when we make choices, moments when we want to get married, and so on. Each one of us has a complex emotional history.

It is also important to recall our *spiritual* history, the history of our relationship with Jesus. When was that moment, that precious moment when you sensed that you are loved? Maybe it was a moment in one of our churches, or you might have simply been praying with your family, or maybe you were simply walking outside and suddenly there was a moment of belief that Jesus lives, that he loves you, and that you are important to him!

I offer you these questions and encourage you to reflect on your deepest desire, to recall your spiritual history, and to rest in your belief that Jesus loves you.

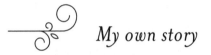 *My own story*

I have my own story of meeting Jesus, my story of important moments. One of the important moments in my life, which I only discovered a number of years later, took place when I was thirteen years old. I had been in France with my family when the German army invaded France. We fled with other refugees and went to Canada. At thirteen, in 1942, I felt a desire to join the armed forces, specifically, the navy. I talked to my dad, asking him if I could do so even if it meant that I had to go back to the United Kingdom, traveling across the Atlantic Ocean by ship. At that time, many ships were being sunk in the Atlantic Ocean. I remember him asking me, "Tell me why you want to go?" I forget what I answered, but I remember what he said: "I trust you. If that is what you want, that is what you must do. I trust you." I think that the fact that he trusted me gave me the chance to trust myself; the very fact that he accepted my intuition to join the navy allowed me to know that my intuitions and desires were trustworthy. This was a very important moment for me. My father, whom I respected, trusted me! I hope that each one of you, at one moment in your lives, has heard someone say to you, "I trust you. I trust your desires." I am praying and hoping that at one moment during our time together, you will hear Jesus say, "I trust you." May you know that God trusts you and that you are important to him.

For eight years, I served in the armed forces and I was taught the art of war. War is a terrible reality. Where there is war, there is hate, and where there is hate, people are killed. Shortly after the liberation of

Paris, my mother and I had to go back to France to see our family. We were welcomed at the Paris station, and at the same station there were people coming from the concentration camps in Germany. They were men and women who had just been liberated, and they still wore the white and blue striped concentration-camp uniforms. They were like skeletons, the living dead.

I was in Rwanda shortly after the genocide, and I saw the open graves where 700,000 people had been tortured and killed. What human beings can do to other human beings! We must rise up and say, "Never again hatred!" We must do everything we can, so that children and adults are never tortured, hurt, or pushed down. This is the message for Christians: stand up so that no child, no person, for whatever reason, is ever hurt, tortured, denied, or killed in genocide. Our world is a dangerous world where hatred can rise suddenly and explode, leading to torture and death. We must find our place in this world, stand up for the truth, and announce the message of Jesus that every person is important. Each one of us must be committed to children, to people with disabilities, to peacemaking, and to working for peace among tribes and countries.

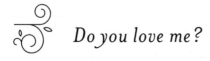 *Do you love me?*

I left the navy in 1950 to follow Jesus. I had to follow his incredible message: not to work for war but for peace, to find ways of seeking peace. After leaving the navy, I had the privilege of visiting a community in France that was founded by a priest who taught me about prayer. I learned that prayer is not just a matter of recitation of words, but it is about being in communion with Jesus, staying with him, resting in him and letting him rest in me. This is the heart of everything, to rest in Jesus and to get to know him.

This was the beginning of my vocation in L'Arche. I was introduced to people with disabilities, who at the time were living in an institution. Theirs was a constant question, "Do you love me?" I later realized that in the Gospel Jesus asks the same question: "Do you love me?" It was at this point that I discovered that people with disabilities, those who have been hurt, rejected, looked down upon, and sometimes tortured, those who have been pushed away, locked up in institutions, and who are not listened to with respect and love, have this same cry, "Do you love me?" This touched me and called me forth as I realized that in their cry there is also the cry of Jesus, "Do you love me?"

Remember the two questions that Jesus asks at the beginning of the Gospel of John: "What are you looking for?" and "What is your desire?" My hope is that you will take time to allow the desire to rise. In the seventh chapter of John there is a beautiful text of Jesus at a Jewish feast. It says that Jesus stood up and cried out, "Let he who thirsts come to me and drink." The question for us then is, What are we thirsting for? All I know is that those who are weak and poor are thirsty for relationships. So the question then becomes, Where is your thirst that will give you the motivation to work for the kingdom?

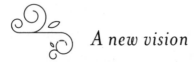 *A new vision*

We are going to discover that Jesus has come to completely change our vision, to give us a new vision of the world.

The message of Jesus is to announce who God is. Jesus also came to announce that, whatever their culture, whatever their abilities or disabilities, whatever their gender, whatever their religion, every person is precious. Every person is unique, and each is important to God and to humanity. Jesus came to reveal the true face of God; he came to reveal the love of God for every person, whatever their abilities or disabilities. Each of those hidden away because of their disabilities, even if they are not recognized by their family, their culture, or society—they are precious to God.

# CHAPTER 2

# The Cry of the Poor

Then the man and his wife heard the sound of the Lord God as he was walking in the garden in the cool of the day, and they hid from the Lord God among the trees of the garden.

But the Lord God called to the man, "Where are you?"

He answered, "I heard you in the garden, and I was afraid because I was naked; so I hid."

(FROM GENESIS 3)

I started L'Arche because I heard the cry of the poor. The cry of the poor is, "Do you see me as important? Am I of value?" The underlying cry of the poor is, "Do you love me?" At the very end of the Gospel of John, Jesus asks Peter the same question, "Do you love me?" By asking this, Jesus shows his vulnerability and his need for love. Jesus teaches us that he is one with the poor.

A few years ago, we welcomed Eric into our community. Eric has his own story, which began with a lot of pain. When his mother discovered the seriousness of his disability, she was devastated and heartbroken; she did not want a child like him! Both mother and Eric were wounded. His mother kept him at home until the age of four, but she did not know what to do with her little boy. Eric was not growing like other children his age, and he was also deaf and blind. At this tender age of four, his mother took him to the local hospital, where it was recommended that he be put into the regional psychiatric hospital. This is where we found Eric twelve years later. He was sixteen years old.

Eric was blind and deaf. He could not speak. He could not walk, and he had a severe intellectual disability. His mother had only come to see him once because she could not bear the lack of love and care that she saw in the hospital. I can say that I have never met a young person so vulnerable and with so much anguish. Eric was living with so much inner pain, yet within that pain lay a mystery.

Eric had not been baptized when he joined our community, but we still took him to the chapel. I remember him sitting in there, in his fragility, blindness, and deafness. There was a quietness about him, and his face was filled with peace. Did he know that he was in the chapel? He may not have known, but it seemed evident that God was present in him.

When Jesus announced the Last Judgment and told the people to come into his kingdom, he said: "When I was naked you clothed me." The crowd responded, "But we never saw you." Jesus continued, "When I was hungry you gave me food." Again, the crowd responded, "But we never saw you." It is clear that the entrance into the kingdom is through compassion, through clothing the naked, welcoming the foreigner, and visiting the prisoner; it is through welcoming the vulnerability of Eric.

Each one of us was born as a little child. This is an incredible reality in our forgotten histories. When a baby is born, the baby is vulnerable, easily wounded, fragile, and without any kind of defense. This child, held lovingly in the arms of the mother, learns through the tone of her voice, the tenderness of her touch, and her unfailing attention that he or she is loved. The child is not frightened of being vulnerable; he or she learns that it is okay to be weak and to have no defenses because he or she knows, *I am loved*. The message of the mother who says, in some way, "You are unique, I love you, you are precious, you are important," is a source of joy for the child.

What happens if a child does not hear this? What happens if the child is caught up in a world of conflict, of hate, and of fear? Such is the vulnerable and broken heart of Eric. The anguish of Eric arose as he sensed that he was not wanted, that he was alone and unloved. We can understand his mother's pain and the pain of parents who discover that their son or daughter has a severe disability. How will a mother in pain gradually discover that it is okay to be the mother of a child like this? To be the mother of Eric?

At the beginning of his life at L'Arche, Eric was incontinent, so one of the first things we did was to try and help him urinate in the toilet. One day he did! We all had champagne that day. People came in and asked what we were celebrating, and we said, "Today Eric has peed in the toilet!" Life is made up of little things. You do not have to do big things to celebrate together in joy. Every morning, one of us living with Eric would give him his bath. Even though he was sixteen, he was small. Bath time was a very precious moment. Through the touch involved in bathing Eric, we helped him to relax and to discover that he was loved.

Over the last few years, I have felt growing within me the recognition of the incredible vulnerability of Jesus, the wounded heart of Christ. The heart of Jesus is wounded because of his yearning to bring us together despite the fact that we are often resistant. The wounded heart of Eric and the wounded heart of Jesus are one. So what is L'Arche about? L'Arche exists to say to the Erics of the world, "I am glad you exist. I am happy to live with you."

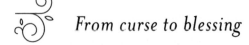

## *From curse to blessing*

I was in Lithuania recently, giving a retreat to parents of people with disabilities. A mother gave the following witness: "When my daughter was born, I was so wounded, it seemed to me that we had been cursed. I asked why this had happened to us." She said that as her daughter grew up, they had to take public transportation, but the way people looked at her and at her daughter, with eyes of curiosity and rejection, made her want to kill herself. One day she went into a church and found there a group of people praying, singing, and dancing. She saw very quickly that many of them had disabilities, and she joined the little group, a Faith and Light community. She said, "From that moment, the curse became a benediction." Through love and solidarity, the malediction was transformed into a blessing!

People sometimes say to me, "You are doing a good job." Well, I am not interested in doing a good job. Instead, I am interested in having fun and in celebrating life together with others, not being caught up in a world of competition or humiliation. We cannot change the world, but we can create places where we celebrate life, where we can give thanks that we are living together as human beings in a beautiful world.

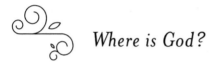 *Where is God?*

The big question for me is still, Where is God? Where is God manifest? Living all these years with people with severe disabilities, people who are vulnerable and fragile, I have discovered the presence of God. I have met Jesus. I have discovered the incredible vulnerability of God.

There is a beauty and vulnerability in each person. As I begin to understand a little of your history and pain, I begin to know your beauty. As we recognize each person's beauty, we can say to one another, "You are more beautiful than you dare believe." We can begin to reveal to the other the presence of God within each one of us.

I was speaking recently to a chaplain of a prison in the United Kingdom. The prison houses men and a few women who have committed serious crimes. It also serves as a psychiatric hospital for the mentally ill. I asked the chaplain that day, "What have you learned about human beings during the time you have been in this mental hospital?" She replied that she had read all of the inmates' files, particularly the ones of those who had committed murder. She said that the majority of them had been abused physically and sexually in their childhoods.

If a child is not loved, what happens? The child has to protect himself or herself in some way. If you are not seen as a person, you will not be able to see others as persons. If you are not regarded with love, you will not be able to look upon others with love; you will just build walls to protect yourself! This is the story of each person. Each of us has personal walls and pain. The yearning of Jesus is to traverse these walls. His vulnerability lies in waiting for the walls of our hearts to come down in the presence of love, and for peace to enter.

## ⌒ *The secret of life*

What is the secret of life that Jesus came to reveal to us—the two fundamental realities of the Gospel? The first is that God is incredibly loving: he is gentle, tender, merciful, and forgiving, and we should not fear him. The second is that every person is precious; every person is important: the Erics of the world, the Samaritans, the Jews, the Romans, the Greeks, the high priests—everyone, no matter their ethnic origin, culture, religion, or occupation.

Jesus's desire is to bring everyone together. But we are all afraid.

Not too long ago, we had a meeting of assistants in our community in France. We talked about fear. We asked everyone to say what his or her greatest fear is. We spoke about our fears: the fear of failure, the fear of not being loved, the fear of death, the fear of disintegration, and the fear of terrible loneliness. It is important for people to speak, to share about their fears. Do not be afraid to give voice to your fears. The danger lies in letting our fears control us and in not learning to walk with them. Our fears may not be eliminated, but we do not have to be controlled by them. We can be in anguish, but we need not be controlled by anguish. It is important to put a finger on our fears and then to hear Jesus say, "Do not be afraid."

## Jesus loves me as I am

I will tell you the story of a little boy of eleven who had an intellectual disability and who was making his First Communion in a parish in France.

It was beautiful, and after the liturgy of the Eucharist, there was a family celebration. During this celebration, the uncle of the little boy, who was also his godfather, went up to his mother and said, "Wasn't it a beautiful liturgy? The only sad thing is that he didn't understand anything." The little boy overheard his uncle and, with tears in his eyes, said to his mother, "Do not worry, Mummy. Jesus loves me as I am." I imagine that the little boy thought: Jesus loves me as I am. I do not have to be different from what I am. I do not have to be what my uncle wants me to be. I do not have to be what mummy would have wanted me to be. I do not even have to be what I would have liked to be. Jesus does not care about my disability. We all have disabilities. Jesus loves me as I am.

We all have disabilities. However, if like this little boy I discover that I'm loved as I am, even with my disability, then my life becomes a question of growing into that greater love.

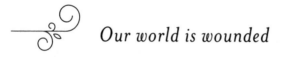 *Our world is wounded*

I can tell you that living with Eric has been a benediction for me. We are healed as we accept those we have rejected. Jesus, just like Eric, is asking, "Do you love me?" This is the same way the wounded, the broken, and the rejected ask, "Do you love me?"

This love is not the same as an emotional affair. To love someone is to reveal to them that they are precious; it is to listen to them. Our world is wounded. Jesus came in his vulnerability to bring people together with their differences. Each one of us, with our different cultures and different languages, is important. Each one is of value, whatever our abilities, disabilities, or culture.

Let me also tell you about Robert. We welcomed Robert many years ago into our little community in Kampala, Uganda. Robert was found in the jungle having been brought up by animals. The result was that he did not walk in an entirely human way and he was a screamer. The military found him, took him to a hospital, and eventually Robert ended up in our community. Up until the time that Robert came to us, he had not been touched or held as a human being. He had not been loved. Nobody had ever said to him, "I love you and you are precious to me." We do not know Robert's entire story, but gradually, as he has continued to live with us, he has begun to discover what it is to be human. A transformation has occurred as Robert slowly realizes that he is loved.

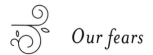 *Our fears*

I would like to cite a text from Genesis, one of the oldest books about the origin of humanity. As you know, in the story of Genesis, God created man and woman as different, but also similar. Man needs woman, and vice versa. To become fully man or fully woman, there is a need to be together and to love each other. There is a need to reveal to the other that they are important, that what they say is of value and that they are listened to. There is need to love with tenderness and to listen with wisdom.

Going back to Genesis, do you remember the moment when the man and woman turn away from God, who goes to look for them? When God finds them, he asks, "Adam, where are you?" and Adam responds, "I was frightened because I was naked and so I hid." This may be the story of each one of us. We, too, turn away from God, but he still comes looking for us.

What is my fear? I may fear that you will see who I am in my poverty, that you will see how fragile I am, or that I have a lot of anguish within me. The result will be that I will fall into loneliness and hide. Where will I hide? I will hide behind power, behind possessions, and behind walls of difference. Hidden behind my walls, I will pretend that I am better than you. I am afraid to show you who I am in my vulnerability, so I hide.

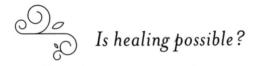 *Is healing possible?*

A few days ago, we celebrated the fortieth anniversary of the death of Dr. Martin Luther King Jr. He was one of the greatest men in history. He was deeply wounded by the way his people were being treated, and he dared to speak out. Some people, when they speak out, are murdered. This is what happened to Jesus as well: he spoke the truth and he was killed. Why don't people want the truth? We don't want the truth because we are afraid of it.

Someone once asked Martin Luther King if it will always be this way, that one group despises the other.

Is it possible for humanity to come together in peace? In today's world, is it possible for the walls to come down so that we can say to one another, "I love you as you are," and "You are precious with your story and with all your hopes"? Will we always be elitist, thinking that we are better than others? Will we always hide behind walls of superiority so that we never really have to listen, thinking that we are better when in reality we are not?

The question that Dr. King was asked is important. Will it always be like this? Will humanity always be at war? What can be done? Reiterating what Jesus said, King responded by teaching that, until we have accepted, recognized, and loved what is broken in us and what is despicable in us, we will continue to despise others. King said, essentially, I must accept myself as a broken person so that peace can come into my heart and into the world.

# ✑◯ *The healing of the poor*

Living in L'Arche with people with severe disabilities has touched many things in me. I have felt the joy of love, but I have also had to question my own values. It is only when I begin to discover my need to pretend that I am superior, that I can begin to see what is broken in me. It is only then that I can enter into a relationship of mutual communion of hearts.

One example of this is with Eric. It is not only a question of doing things for him; this is of course important; but it is just a beginning. It is also important for him to meet my heart, for us to become vulnerable to each other, for us to learn to admit to each other that we are both fragile and vulnerable and that we have been brought together.

Jesus became flesh. "To become flesh" is a very strong expression. Jesus did not just become a human being; he did not just become a man; he became flesh. Flesh is fragile; it moves and it is vulnerable. Jesus became vulnerable. We, however, are afraid of the vulnerability of Jesus, so we reject him, perpetuating division, and avoiding communion of hearts. The message Jesus gives us is that he has come to give us a new reality: that we can accept ourselves as we are in our brokenness. And when this happens, it is possible to accept one another. And then the walls can come down.

The question remains, Is this something true, or is it an idealistic situation? Did Jesus really come to change my heart of stone into a heart of flesh? Is it really true that those that I reject are those who can heal me if I accept them, if I listen to them? I think this is our story at L'Arche: that the Erics and the Roberts of the world can heal us. Can this be true? Can the Gospel be true? I can say from the witnesses of L'Arche and Faith and Light communities that yes, it is true. However, I cannot say that I am healed. I can only say that I am on a road of healing. I cannot say that I am transformed. I can only say that I am on a road of transformation. I believe that it is the Erics and the Roberts and many others like them around the world who have the capacity to heal us.

CHAPTER 3

# *The Feast Is Ready*

When you give a lunch, do not invite your friends, or your rich neighbors; for they will invite you back and in this way you will be paid for what you did.

When you give a feast, invite the poor, the lame, and the blind, and you will be happy.

(FROM LUKE 14)

I am not here to tell you that L'Arche is a good place. I am here to announce a vision that has been opened to us through the poor in our lives. The vision is that God is present in the weakest and in the most vulnerable. In L'Arche, we welcome the weak and the vulnerable in the sense that we recognize them as important. We meet each one of them as human beings, without despising them, without looking down on them, and without feeling that we are superior. When we do this, we enter a process of transformation, into a vision of the world where there can be peace. I know change has to begin with me. I have to change. I have to grow in accepting people with their differences.

 *Janine*

Janine came into our community about thirty years ago. She was forty years old at the time, had epilepsy, was a hemophiliac, and was also paralyzed in one arm and one leg. When she came to us, Janine was full of violence and rage. She would break things and scream.

When someone is violent in our community, we try to understand the reason why. We do not try to stop the violence first, but instead, we sit down with the person and ask, "Tell me, where is your pain?" At that time we had a very good psychiatrist, and together, we tried to understand Janine. We came to realize that people with disabilities have suffered much rejection, that they have a part of their being that has been severely broken. They may also have psychotic tendencies and may need medication.

In a way, it was not difficult to understand Janine's violence. Her family did not want her anymore; her mother had died, and her sisters could not keep her. Perhaps her greatest pain was being unable to bear children. Janine needed to express her anger with God, with her family, and with her body. When Janine is violent, I say, "I understand it is not easy for you. The rejection you have lived with could not have been easy for you. It must be difficult to accept the fact that you cannot bear a child. I understand." People often feel guilty if they are violent, even when their violence is natural and normal. It is important for us to acknowledge the violence within ourselves so that we can say to Janine and others, "I understand." We must accept ourselves as people who are broken.

I remember I was asked to talk to a forty-year-old mother who was eight months pregnant and who had discovered that her baby would be born with a severe handicap. When I met her, she was in tears and close to hysteria. All I could say was, "I understand your anger." I understand that, at forty, a woman might not have another child.

It is important to understand the violence of people and why they close themselves up in depression. When this happens, the next step is to figure out what to do. Janine gradually learned to talk. She had always been able to talk, but she had to find her own voice. People must talk to others about their pain, about their violence, and we must try to understand. Janine worked in our workshop, but like a lot of people she did not enjoy the work. Slowly but surely, however, we discovered that one of her gifts was an ability to sing. Janine sung the old songs of Paris, which she loved, songs which no one else could sing. Slowly but surely, she discovered that she had a gift and a place. It would take many years, but gradually Janine discovered that she was loved.

One day Janine asked to be baptized. In our community we do not push people to believe in Jesus; we let it happen naturally. Jesus knows what to do, so we do not push. It is important that a person does not ask to be baptized just to please us, but to please Jesus, and so Janine's request came. Why? Something was coming up within her. She had lived an experience with Jesus, and she had a desire to know him better. She was able to make an important choice. In our community, we help people to have desires and to make choices.

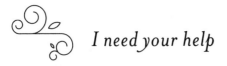 *I need your help*

Janine chose to live in another home. We live in several little homes, and she chose a different one from the one she had been living in. A few years later, she became angry again, this time because her body had become too heavy for her legs to hold. Janine needed a wheelchair, and she also needed someone to give her a shower or a bath and to help her dress. The idea of becoming more dependent made Janine angry. It took some time for her to discover that, as she grew weaker, she had to be able to say, "I cannot do it by myself. I need you."

When I turned seventy, the people with disabilities with whom I share a home said to me, "You should not do the cleaning up anymore." It is wonderful to become seventy! One does not have to do the cleaning up! The people that I live with have understood that I need help. To say, "I need your help," is at the heart of community. In L'Arche, we are discovering that "I need you" is indeed the heart of the Church.

St. Paul said that those parts of the Church that are the least presentable and the weakest are indispensable in the Church. We need to deepen our understanding of this truth: that the Church needs people with disabilities. The whole mystery lies in being able to accept that we are weak, to say, "I cannot do it by myself. I need Jesus. I need your help. I need the Church and I need the word of God." We must be people who are able to say, "I need you," and not people who think that we can do everything on our own. The truth is that we cannot. Community is about building a body, and we all need one another. Weakness is about accepting who we are, accepting our vulnerabilities and our poverty.

## ∽◯ *What are we seeking?*

In the sixties, the question young students asked was: What sort of society do we want? Today, this is no longer the question. The question has now become: How do we succeed in a society that has developed through global communication, through the desire for money, power, and progress?

I have heard that many young people in Kenya are looking for the four-by-four dream: a four-year university education, a family of four (husband, wife, and two children), a house with four rooms, and a four-wheel-drive car. Of course, when you have a society based on competition, right from the basic level of school, accentuated by television and an entire economy, this is likely to happen. Some will win, some will lose, and many will be victims. Today there exists a double world with a growing gap between the rich and the poor—an issue that was a deep concern for Jesus. This gap existed even in his time. There have always been more and more people who are dissatisfied, seeking ways of finding money.

We have to face the fact that we live in a society full of competition, one that has been built on economics. In a globalized reality we have to see what is happening and to see where the place of Jesus is, as the world moves from a society of culture to a society of competition. We must be wise, and we must be united in weakness—our own, and that of our brothers and sisters.

I was told that, during the inception of the community of Saint Martin, a survey was carried out, and in an area of about fifty square kilometers, two thousand people with disabilities were found, hidden away. What does this mean for the Church? What vision do we have for people with disabilities? My feeling is that we are not here just to create nice little institutions for them; rather, we are here to help them discover that they have an important place in the world, in the Church.

I feel sad and wounded when I hear people say, "God cannot exist, because there is too much pain in this world," as if it is God's fault. We know that it is not God's fault; it is the fault of all of us. If someone is hungry and the food available is not enough, we have to learn to share. We human beings have been given a beautiful responsibility: to build something new. We are invited to move from a closed culture to the realization that every person is important, that every person should have a place in the Church and in the society. This is a responsibility and invitation that has immense implications for all of us.

## Love frees us from fear

When Jesus started to announce the Good News, he revealed little by little, through signs, that he was the Messiah. Many people, including a number of the apostles, felt that Jesus had come to liberate Israel and to throw the Romans out the door. This was the expectation and vision that many of the Jewish people had in Jesus's time, that the Messiah would come and give the Jewish people back their dignity. They were, however, disappointed because this is not quite what Jesus wanted. He wanted to liberate each one of us: to liberate us from selfishness and from being closed up in ourselves, to rid our hearts of hatred. Jesus came to transform us and to liberate us from being controlled and governed by fear: the fear of sickness, the fear of failure, the fear of being pushed down, the fear of not being loved, the fear of loneliness, fears that will remain within each one of us. How does he do this? Jesus frees us by saying to each one of us, "I love you."

There is a beautiful text from the book of Revelation, where the Lord says, "I stand and knock at the door. If somebody hears me and opens the door, I will enter and I will eat with that person and that person will eat with me." In biblical language, to eat with someone is to enter into a covenant relationship with that person; it is to become a friend of that person. There is a proverb that says, to become a friend of someone, you have to eat a sack of salt together. To eat together is a revelation. It announces that two people are friends. I am amazed at the humility of Jesus, who says, "I stand at the door and knock. If somebody hears me. . . ." Maybe we do not want to hear him. We have too much going on in our heads, too many projects, too much anguish and fear, fear of what people think, fear of not being accepted. Jesus does not knock the door down; he just humbly knocks and he waits, vulnerable to our indifference and rejection.

 *The feast is ready*

The vulnerability of Jesus is also portrayed in an incredible parable that he gives us in the twenty-second chapter of Matthew, on the marriage feast. The meaning behind it is very important. The parable is about a king who prepares a wedding feast. When everything is ready, he sends his servants to all the people of the town and says, "Come, the wedding feast is ready." Their response is, "Sorry, I am too busy. I have short-term projects to complete so I cannot come." Short-term projects in the Gospel refer to projects like trying out a couple of oxen, buying land to build on, or marrying off a daughter. All these are projects that enhance social position, power, and wealth. In a culture based on competition, where each person is trying to win, people do not have time. This hurts the king, who feels rejected. His wounds are like the vulnerability of Jesus. The king and Jesus each offer something incredible. The king offers a feast, and Jesus offers a vision of peace, of bringing people together, of celebration, and of unity: a new vision. We, on the other hand, are all too busy to accept either invitation. We do not let ourselves be formed and transformed by Jesus. We refuse to grow in wisdom, to become more human, and to become more loving.

## Jesus wants to become my friend

All Jesus wants is to become my friend. To be his friend means to let Jesus: come and live within me. This is the whole vision of Jesus, to bring people together, people who are different, people who are closed up in a culture where they desire more power, more money, more leisure, and more comfort. What then is our vision? As in the community of Saint Martin, where it was found that around two thousand people with disabilities in the area had been hidden, what do we do? Where is our vision? How do we advance the vision we have discovered? This is the dilemma.

In Leviticus, we read that in biblical times people with leprosy were put aside. This was because leprosy was seen as a disorder of creation. Sometimes I hear it said that people with disabilities are a disorder of creation. Little by little, though, through the prophets, the vision is revealed: people with disabilities are important. They are human beings, and they should be looked upon and treated with respect.

St. Francis said, "I had always been afraid of people with leprosy and held them in horror." During that period, the Middle Ages in Europe, there were about twenty thousand leprosy centers where people with leprosy were closed in groups. Leprosy created fear because, at that time, there was no medication, it was contagious, and those parts of the body affected would be eaten away by the disease. In time, Francis said, "One day, I was led into a leprosarium and I spent time with the lepers. When I left them, there was a new gentleness within my body and spirit." Something new—a gentleness—welled up within him. So, having been with the lepers, he was transformed. St. Francis says that it was from that moment that he followed the Lord.

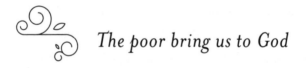 *The poor bring us to God*

Not long ago, within our community of Faith and Light in Syria, I gave a talk to people who were mainly of the Muslim faith. There were mothers and fathers, and a few hundred others. When the supreme mufti got up to thank me, he said, "If I understand you correctly, you are saying that if you get closer to people with disabilities, they will lead you to God." I replied, "Yes, this is the mystery."

If we get close to those who are rejected, to those we feel superior to, if we meet these people as it happened in the parable of the wedding feast, with the king who brought in the poor, the disabled, and the blind for a free meal, then we become a community, at the heart of which is the mystery of our communion with Jesus. St. Paul says that God has chosen the weak of this world to confound the strong. He has chosen the foolish to confound the so-called clever. In other words, God has chosen the most despised—Janine, Eric, Robert, and others I have talked of—to transform the rest.

I have already mentioned that my first encounter with people with disabilities was in an institution in France. I remember when I became a part of the institution. My spiritual father told me that to understand human beings, to understand a society that excludes certain people, to understand the message of Jesus, I had to meet people with disabilities and to listen to what they had to say. I was of course a bit nervous, wondering how I would speak with those who do not speak, with those who do not hear. I did not have any understanding yet of what they were living, and so

I asked, "What can we talk about? What can I share about?" What surprised me, thrilled me, and what I found beautiful, was that each one's cry was not for knowledge or power, but for relationship. As mentioned earlier, the question each one asked of me was, "Do you want to become my friend? Do you love me? Will you come back to see me?" Their desire was not for power, not for social standing, not for money, but for relationship, a yearning that Jesus shares.

Those who are brought up in a society full of competition and closed in a world fed by the media will find it difficult to understand the God of relationships, the one who declares, "He who eats my body and drinks my blood, lives in me and I live in him." Jesus has a vision for our world, to bring people together in love. There is a beautiful text found in the second chapter of Ephesians. St. Paul says, Jesus is our peace; he has made us all one. Here, Paul is talking about the culture of the Jews and that of the Greeks, who are extremely different from each other. The Jews were confident of the fact that they were much better than the Greeks, and vice versa, and yet they became one. Paul says that our relationship with Jesus has broken down the dividing wall of hostility, the walls that we put up between cultures and between people.

## ❧ *Becoming friends*

I can be generous: I can volunteer to help someone living in an institution, or I can go into a slum area and listen to people, or give them money. However, when I am generous, I hold the power. In my generosity, I give good things when I want. The initiative is mine. When I extend my generosity to you, I become superior. The equation changes, however, when I become your friend. The generosity becomes a meeting point for the two of us, and the journey of friendship begins. When I become your friend, I become vulnerable to you. When I am vulnerable with you, I listen to your story; I hear how much you have suffered; and you listen to my story. In some mysterious way, friendship is the beginning of a covenant whereby we are all tied to one another. You have to know that once you become the friend of someone with disabilities, much of your life begins to change.

True friendship is described in the beautiful parable of Jesus, the one of the good Samaritan. A young student of Mosaic law comes to Jesus and asks, "Who is my neighbor?" Jesus answers by telling the parable of the Jewish man who gets beaten up and all his money is stolen as he travels from Jerusalem to Jericho. This man is lying on the ground, and two religious Jewish people pass by, see him, and move on because they are afraid. They are governed by fear. The two religious Jews are followed by a Samaritan, who sees the man lying on the ground. He stops and takes out a bottle of wine to clean and disinfect his wounds. Then he applies oil to help the healing process. He then puts the injured man onto his donkey and takes him to the local hotel, and there he spends the night beside him. You have to remember that the Samaritans were considered enemies of the Jewish people; they were seen as inferior and of no value, but here we see a competent man who knows what he is doing, someone who is not emotional. When the Jewish man realizes that the one who has rescued him is a Samaritan, he experiences something new in his heart. The same is experienced by the Samaritan, who is moved from generosity to a meeting, from assistance to a covenant. The two have now become bonded; they love each other. Then Jesus says to his disciples and to the young man, "Go and do likewise." Jesus tells us to become a friend.

## Invite the poor and you will be happy

In Luke 14, Jesus says, when you give a meal, do not invite the members of your family. Do not invite your friends or your rich neighbors. Do not invite the clan, the people you are always with. Instead, invite the poor, the lame, the blind, and you will be happy. Friendship can be a beautiful reality, but it can also be full of pain. Friendship can provide a place where we can spend our time, flattering each other about our physical appearance, a way of closing ourselves up, but it can also be true friendship where we spend time together, where we open ourselves up, where we become peacemakers in this world, where we bring people who are different together. Jesus does not say, "If you invite the poor to your table, they will be blessed because they will have received some good food." No, he says instead that *you* will be blessed.

You will begin to change when you become a friend to someone who has been marginalized, someone who has been an enemy. As I welcome you, the marginalized or the person with disabilities, to enter into friendship with me, something changes within me. In our relationship, I begin to touch what is broken in me.

# CHAPTER 4

# *To Live in Unity*

Now in Christ Jesus you who once were far off have become close through the blood of Christ.

For he is our peace. He broke down the wall of enmity that was dividing two different people so that he might create in himself one new person in place of the two.

(FROM EPHESIANS 2)

My teachers have been people with disabilities. Maimuna and Dorothy are among these teachers, and they live in the L'Arche community in Uganda. Maimuna and Dorothy do not speak much;

they do not work much; but they will tell you something extraordinary. When you look into Maimuna's eyes or listen to Dorothy, what you see and hear is their wholeness, their total acceptance of themselves. As we get close to Maimuna or Dorothy, our little daily complaints disappear. They are so physically broken and yet are whole in their spirits. Maimuna and Dorothy teach me to accept myself as I am, to accept myself as a human being, to accept myself as a child of God, and to accept myself as the beloved of Jesus. This is their secret: Jesus loves us, and it does not matter how much we have studied or what we have done. What is important is that each of us is the beloved of God. From whatever country, culture, religion, background, or history, I'm just me and Jesus loves me.

 *Faith is about transformation*

What is it that transforms me and permits me to accept myself with my history, with the wounds and pain that I have lived with, with my father who was this or that, or with my mother who was this or that, or with the fact that I was or was not loved as a child? Each one of us is carrying a lot of pain. We try to hide this pain, sometimes even through spirituality. I remember this woman I once met. She was always speaking about Jesus, and this touched me, but one day she slipped and she started to tell me about her depression. I would rather she had spoken straightaway about her depression instead of hiding it. Sometimes we can hide things, using Jesus as a screen without having a relationship with him. However, when we have a relationship with Jesus, we come to understand that we are known and loved by him as we are.

Everything in faith is about transformation: accepting my history, accepting my depression, and accepting my violence. I have to accept that I have violence in me, that I am depressed, and it is something I have to work on. I have to understand where it comes from and how this energy can be transformed. Acceptance is a work in progress. The beautiful thing is that Jesus and our brothers and sisters walk with us on this journey.

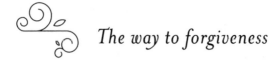

# The way to forgiveness

I gave a retreat to some contemplative sisters in Indonesia. After the retreat, we met for a short question-and-answer moment, and one of them said to me, "I have hated one of my sisters so much I wanted to kill her! What must I do with this?" I replied, "You are special. It is amazing that you are able to talk about it. Do not hold your anger inside." What I found wonderful was that she was able to speak freely about her anger.

When I was the leader in my community, I would sometimes ask all the male assistants to tell me about their violence. This is a part of our reality. We all have "darkness" within us. We have all been terribly hurt and wounded. Our parents may have loved us, but they may also have hurt us in some ways. Maybe my father was an alcoholic and my relationship with men has been twisted because of this first relationship. My mother may have loved me but she may have hurt me, too. The whole struggle becomes how to accept myself as I am with all my pain and all my beauty.

## ⌒◯ *From hatred to understanding*

Once a young girl came to talk to me. She said many things, but as I listened, I felt that she had a lot of anger toward men. I stopped her at one moment and said, "Can I ask you a question?" She said yes, so I asked, "Tell me about your relationship with your father," and she blurted out: "I hate him!" I felt I needed to hear more, so I asked again, "Can you tell more more?" She said, "My father teaches religion in a Catholic school. The religious authorities admire him and speak well of him, but when he comes home he locks himself in his room with his books, never eating with us. He has never spoken to me and I hate him." We did not have much time, but it was important that she was able to talk about it. If I had had more time, I would have asked her what the relationship of her father to his father was like. I am pretty sure she would have said that there had been no relationship, that perhaps her father's father was an alcoholic, or that he was this or the other, and I would have been able to say, "Your dad cannot have a relationship with you because he did not have one with his father. He does not know how to be a father." There could have been a moment when she would have said, "Oh. I understand." That is how to move from hatred to understanding, and from understanding to compassion. It is a road of forgiveness.

We have to enter into a process of forgiveness, that long process which is the process of liberation. We must learn to forgive ourselves and to forgive others. It is a long process because we are fragile, wounded people who must somehow learn to accept the wounds that are within us— particularly if we were not loved as children, if we were not desired, or if we were sexually abused. We need to enter into a process of liberation from our wounds.

## The long journey to forgiveness

During my visit to Rwanda after the genocide, I remember listening to a woman who told me that seventy-five members of her family had been assassinated. She was carrying a lot of hate in her heart, and she said to me, "I do not know what to do." I said, "I understand."

Forgiveness is a long journey and transformation an even longer one. They both happen slowly but surely. I asked this woman from Rwanda if she wanted to kill those who had killed her family, and she said, "No! There is enough death around!" I then asked her whether she was aware that the first step in the process of forgiveness is not vengeance, but rather, a need to talk about what happened. The heart of the message of Jesus is to love your enemy, but we need to remember that forgiveness is a long journey and not just a spiritual thing. We are human beings with wounded hearts, and we must take care of our hearts. We are always reminded that we are more human than divine than we dare to believe. We have human hearts that need to be loved and to love, but we are also temples of the divine. This is how we make the passage to transformation.

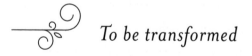 *To be transformed*

During my time in Kenya I have heard some people say that they were taught, right from childhood, that their tribe was the best. They were brought up with the reality of elitism, disdain, and hatred. This is also the history of slavery, the history of humanity. The history of slavery is terrible. I am not only referring to the slavery that led to people being taken from West Africa to America, but rather, all forms of slavery. The Jewish people were also slaves. So many structures throughout history have been built by slaves, who in turn were starved, hurt, and tortured. The history of slavery is that of elitism and hatred. We close ourselves up in our group and close our eyes and hearts to the suffering of others.

We need to hear again the incredible words of Jesus in Luke 14: "When you give a meal, do not invite the members of your family. Do not invite your friends and do not invite your rich neighbors." This is to say, do not invite your clan, the group of people you are always with and with whom we are always saying we're the best, and we are the ones who know best. The greatest danger is that we will hide behind our prejudices, where we will think that we are better than others, that we are the ones who know, because along with this elitism will come hatred.

If you read any books on the saints, you will discover that as one grows in spirituality, one feels less and less perfect. So, if you are feeling less and less perfect, it means that you are getting close to God! Those in religious life, when they entered the novitiate, had wings. After that, the wings were clipped and they began living in community, a life they found painful. I have done it for five decades and survived. I hear the same thing about family life: it begins beautifully, with the honeymoon, and then after some years there is a breakdown in communication. So it was for the woman who lived with the pain of giving birth to a disabled child, a pain that remained for many years. Then, one day came her discovery that people like her child, people like Dorothy, Maimuna, and others, can become teachers and that a relationship with them is transformative.

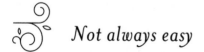 *Not always easy*

To have dinner with the poor, the lame, the marginalized, and the blind is not always a picnic, and we have experienced this in L'Arche. Suddenly in the middle of a meal, Janine can get up and start screaming, which is okay for her—she needs to get it out. But for people who are not used to it, it can be a bit too much to handle. I remember one day I had invited somebody "quite important" from Paris to visit our community. Fortunately, he was an open person, because on this particular day someone else had prepared the places at the table, and this important man found himself sitting in front of Ivan. Now, Ivan is a man with a severe disability, and when he coughs, he sends things flying onto the plate of the person seated in front of him. I would personally not have placed Ivan in front of this man, but when I came and saw the seating places already arranged, there was nothing much I could do. Ivan of course coughed, and as I said, he aimed for the plate of the person in front of him. Please, do not believe that living with people with disabilities is all filled with love; you never know what to expect! So, take a meal with the poor, the lame, the disabled, knowing that it will not always be a picnic.

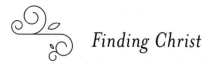 *Finding Christ*

How can God be living in a mysterious way in those who are the broken? We can all kneel before the cross, but we are yet to accept our own cross, a cross that is inscribed in our flesh and in our history. We are people of the cross, but we do not always want to look at it or accept it. Instead, we want to think that we are okay, but we are not. We still have a long road to travel.

Jesus came to bring peace. St. Paul in Ephesians says, "Jesus is our peace." Destroying in his flesh the dividing walls of hostility, he brings unity and healing. The big crisis in the church, which lasted for many years, was the relationship between the Jews who had become Christians, and the Greeks who had received the Holy Spirit and Baptism. Of course, the Greeks despised the Jews and the Jews despised the Greeks, but finally they came together; they were transformed in the Spirit. Jesus did not come to liberate the Jewish people from the oppression of the Romans; he came to bring peace to our world by transforming me, by changing me. I need to be purified so that I no longer hold on to a culture as if it is the only culture that exists, as if it is my place of security. My security comes from Jesus because he loves me and he has revealed himself to me.

Transformation implies a vision, the Gospel's vision. We must love the Gospels. We must be centered on them. We must take every word of Jesus as the word of God, hold on to it, and see this incredible vision of unity. St. Paul talks about those parts of the body that are the least presentable, the weakest, as those we hide away. The brothers and sisters of Saint Martin found around two thousand people with disabilities hidden away. Theirs is not an isolated case. All over the world the least presentable, the weakest, are hidden away.

So, what is the vision? Is it true that whatever you do to the least of my brothers you do unto me? Is it true that the face of Jesus is in the oppressed and the broken? If it is true, then an immense change is called for. The change is that if you become a friend of the marginalized person, you will become a friend of Jesus, and you will enter a process of transformation.

We must all be centered on the Gospel message, but let's face it: it's not possible. This is why Jesus said that it is easier for a camel to go through the eye of a needle than it is for a rich man to enter the kingdom. This made Peter ask, "God, who can be saved?" We cannot do it, but nothing is impossible with God. We need to let ourselves be transformed. Transformation, however, needs a vision. It needs one to maintain an openness to touch that which needs to be transformed within him or herself. It needs one to touch their hatred, their anger, their own wounds, their nonacceptance of their bodies, and their own story.

## ｅ◯ *To live in unity*

Jesus has a vision of peace and of bringing people together. "That they may become one as the Father and I are one. You in me and I in them." His yearning and vision are that we may become one, that we may love one another because we are all part of an incredibly beautiful humanity, diverse in culture, diverse in religion, diverse in so many ways. Jesus says, "Come together." It is not easy but rather painful. Living with the poor is not always a picnic, but it is a place of healing in a world full of hatred and oppression.

Jesus came to announce the Good News to the poor. What is this announcement of the Good News to the poor? It is simply that you are loved by God, that you are loved by me, that I want to live with you and that you are important. We need to come together from different places and from different cultures. I see this in our community in Calcutta where Muslims, Hindus, and Christians from different denominations live, work, and pray together. Our beautiful little home, given to us by Mother Teresa just next to her Sisters, is a place where we live together and love one another. This does not mean that there is no conflict; in fact there can be more conflict between Catholics themselves than there is conflict between people of different religions. This is because our basic humanity has been wounded by sin, wounded by rejection, wounded by so many elements. In reality, we need one another; we need to touch our wounds and keep the vision. I am wounded. I need help from my community. I need help from Jesus, because I cannot do it on my own.

# ᘒ *My own cross*

Transformation is to gradually discover that I can only move from the wound to the vision because somehow I have had an experience of Jesus, who is saying to me, "Follow me." He is saying to me, "Follow me to the Resurrection, through the Cross." You cannot become a man or woman of peace unless you have touched within you the places of aggression and hatred. If you have not touched these wounds within, you cannot walk to the place of resurrection. We are children of the cross and children of the Resurrection.

It is okay to say, "In the name of the Father and the Son and the Holy Spirit," when you make the sign of the cross. But we cannot stop there. We ought to live the cross. Living the cross as men and women of hope means we have been wounded, but we know we are loved. The vulnerable Jesus is yearning to find disciples who are becoming his friends and who want to work with him to build peace.

# *Option for the poor?*

Those who are the most rejected must be respected. It is not a question of a preferential option for the poor. It is the fact that the Church is constituted by the presence of the poor. The poor are indispensable to the Church, because in their cry for recognition, in their cry for relationships, they are awakening the hearts of those who are seemingly rich in knowledge, wealth, or security. We the Church are being touched to become people of compassion. Deep forces have been called forth from within my heart so that I can welcome you, the broken one. As I welcome you, I discover that I am broken, too. I also discover that Maimuna and Dorothy are my teachers, because those who have been crushed for whatever reason are a sign of the presence of God, and where there is the presence of God, the disciples of Jesus must be present.

# CHAPTER 5

# *Be Open*

The Lord said to me:

Son of man, these bones are the whole house of Israel.

They say, "Our bones are dried up and our hope is gone; we are cut off."

Therefore prophesy and say to them:

"This is what the Lord says: 'O my people, I am going to open your graves and bring you up from them; I will bring you back to the land of Israel.'"

(from Ezekiel 37)

In chapter 37 of Ezekiel, a painful vision is made manifest. Ezekiel talks of a valley, a huge valley, a valley filled with dead, dry bones. How frightening! He must have thought it was a nightmare! In the vision, the Lord God says to Ezekiel, "Son of man, can these bones live?" and Ezekiel the prophet answers, "You alone, Lord, know." Then the Lord God says to Ezekiel, "Prophesy to these bones," and the prophet does.

In this vision, Ezekiel saw the bones coming together, after which, flesh and skin covered them. Before long, a whole lot of people were standing before him, although they had no spirit within them. They stood there like dead bodies. Again, the Lord God said to the prophet: "Prophesy to the spirit," and the prophet Ezekiel did. Suddenly, all the people who appeared dead were filled with life, and an immense multitude of men and women came alive.

After the vision appeared to Ezekiel, the Lord God interpreted it and gave it meaning. The words as they were given to Ezekiel by God went thus: "Son of man, these bones are the whole house of Israel. They have been saying, 'Our bones are dried up, our hope is gone, and we are cut off.'"

Many people throughout the world have a similar cry. They become depressed and discouraged when they see the divisions, the injustices, the immense gap between the rich and the poor and the conflicts that exist in every country. They cry, "We have no more hope! Where is our hope? Our bones are dried up! We have been put aside and we are no good." But the Lord God says to them: "O my people, I am going to open your graves and have you rise from them. You will know that I am the Lord when I open your graves and raise you from them and you shall live. I will place you in your own land and will put my Spirit within you, O my people. Then you will know that I, the Lord, have spoken and have done it." This vision and the resurrection of Jesus say to each one of us: I will take away your discouragement and your despair. I will raise you up, my people, from your graves, the graves of your hearts. I will put my spirit within you, and you will stand up. You will become my people, and you will bring peace to the world.

# Everyone is important

What Jesus wants is to bring people together. We know that in many cultures, people with disabilities are hidden away and put aside. Their parents' hearts are wounded; in one way or another they erroneously believe that their child is a punishment from God. On the contrary, that child, like every child, is beautiful. That child, like every child, is a child of God. We are all different in language and in capacity. Some people are capable whereas others, perhaps by birth or perhaps through illness, are less capable. But everyone is important.

Our role in L'Arche is to say to those who have been put aside, the outcast and the marginalized: You are precious. You are beautiful, and you are loved by God. Stand up, rise up, and trust the Lord our God.

Jesus is not just speaking to the forgotten and to those with disabilities who have been hidden away in houses or in institutions. He is saying to each one of us, "Stand up and discover how beautiful you are." You have a message, a gift to give to the world. In this world where there is corruption, division, and injustice, where there is a great divide between the rich and the poor and where there are armed conflicts, Jesus is sending his messengers. We are all his messengers, empowered to bring peace to our world and to discover that, through love and wisdom, we can build communities of love, signs of peace for our world.

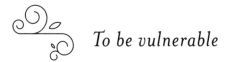 *To be vulnerable*

There is something I would like to delve deeper into with you—something that will help us understand the vision of Jesus for our world and the place of people with severe disabilities in it.

The Gospel of John begins with the incredible prologue where we learn that before all things, the Word existed. "In the beginning was the Word and the Word was with God." You can replace "the Word was with God" with "the Word was in communion with God." Then we learn that the most extraordinary reality, the Word, became flesh. The Word of God, by whom all things were made, became flesh! It does not say "became a human being," but rather, became flesh.

We all have this reality of our flesh. It is something that changes, something fragile and vulnerable. The Word became flesh, which can also be interpreted as "the Word became vulnerable." I understand from this that those people who are vulnerable are the place where God resides. The person who is vulnerable becomes the presence of God.

I share with you my conviction that we need to discover the vulnerability of the heart of Christ, Christ wounded in his heart by our lack of love and lack of openness to this mystery. Together, let us contemplate the mystery of how people who are vulnerable are the presence of God and how Jesus is vulnerable. The whole of the history of humanity through all the cultures asks: Who is God and where is God? In many cultures, there is a fear of God. God had to be placated with sacrifices and his favor sought in order to get good things. We fear God because he can punish us. Jesus came to reveal that we are not to be frightened of God, because God is loving, God is tender, gentle, delicate, and humble.

## ◯ ◯ *God is hidden*

What does Jesus reveal? He reveals, on one side, who God is, and on the other, the mystery of people with disabilities. God is hidden, and people with disabilities are hidden. We do not see him. Where is he? People with disabilities—where are they? Two thousand people with disabilities were hidden away around Nyahururu, a reality that exists in all countries. What is the relationship between people with disabilities and God?

There is a revelation of God and at the same time a revelation of the meaning of the weakest, particularly in our cultures of competition. In a culture of competition, some people win, many lose, and even more are victims. In a culture of competition, those who are vulnerable and weak are seen as a shame. People are ashamed of them.

I gave a retreat to a Faith and Light community, and during Mass, at the time of offering, all the mothers of children with severe disabilities came forward and offered their children. How moving that as the priest offered the host to be consecrated, the mothers were offering their children—children who are a presence of God. After the Eucharistic celebration, we had a meeting. Many of the women were from villages nearby, and I asked them, "What has Faith and Light taught you?" and they replied, "We no longer feel ashamed to have a son or a daughter like this."

## Françoise

When we first welcomed Françoise, who has a severe disability, she was about forty years old. She could not speak and had difficulty feeding herself. She could only manage to walk a little. Thirty years later, and at seventy, she is now blind and can no longer walk at all. All she can do is to cry out a little. Most of the time, she lies in her bed, although sometimes she is brought into the main room. The assistants enter into a relationship with her by giving her a bath and by feeding her.

When I go into that little home, I love to spend a few minutes each time with Françoise. I put my two hands on her face, and I say, "Françoise, it's you," and she is there. She cannot do much, but her greatest cry is for a relationship. If Françoise has no relationship, she will die. The relationship is not about giving her food or washing her body; it is in the way we give her food and the way we touch her body. We touch her body with respect and with love, not to use it, but to honor it. We touch her body because she is the temple of the Holy Spirit and because God lives within her. We touch her body as the body of Christ, with respect.

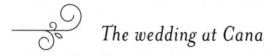 *The wedding at Cana*

At the beginning of John's Gospel, two disciples of John the Baptist leave him to follow Jesus. One of them, Andrew, goes to call his brother and says, "I have found the Messiah." Next on their journey they find Philip, who joins them. Philip then brings a friend, Nathaniel. When they come to Jesus, he says to them, "Come and follow me." So, little by little, a group of believers assembles around Jesus.

Where is Jesus going to take them, these first five found in the Gospel of John? One would think that Jesus would take them into the desert for a sort of retreat; instead, he takes them to a wedding feast! A wedding feast and drinking have the same roots in the language—in other words, people would go to a wedding to drink. In Israel at that time, a wedding lasted for an entire week. This particular wedding was held in a place called Cana in Galilee. People came from all over to attend and to celebrate. I think Jesus, too, went to the wedding because he knew there would be a wonderful time, and he wanted to celebrate. This shows the humanity of Jesus: he loves to celebrate, to sing, and to dance, because that is what we human beings are called to be—to be men and women of celebration!

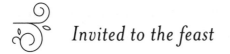

## *Invited to the feast*

I want to explore more deeply why Jesus takes them to a wedding feast, and for that I go to the Gospel of St. Matthew, chapter 22. Here, Jesus says, "The kingdom of God is like a great wedding feast." The kingdom of God is a place of celebration, a community where people love one another and where every person finds their place. To what, then, is Jesus calling us? He is calling us to a banquet of love. You can imagine how upset the king is in this Gospel story when the servants return saying that nobody wants to come to the banquet of love that has been prepared for them.

Maybe for us, attending the banquet of love is difficult because we are frightened of love. Maybe we are all frightened of relationship. We are frightened of entering a relationship of love because we will become vulnerable. Entering into a relationship of love means that I will have to open my heart to you, and as soon as I open my heart to you, I become vulnerable and I can be hurt. We have all experienced love, and maybe we have all experienced rejection. We have entered relationships of love, and we have been wounded, disappointed, and disillusioned.

When people get married, many enter a honeymoon period—a beautiful time when the two share deeply. Ten years down the line, however, communication breaks down. Where has the love gone? Perhaps we are welcomed into a community with great enthusiasm, but ten years later, we become busy and no longer relate; we no longer love each other. In both cases, we are not listening to one another, because we may be frightened of the relationship. Instead, we try to find recognition through doing things and through a sense of power.

 *Community of love*

So, Jesus in the wedding feast parable says to bring to the feast all those who have been excluded, those who have been pushed aside. Bring in all those mothers with severely disabled children. Bring in all those who are not wanted because they are limited in their ability. Bring in all those who are crying out for an authentic, respectful, loving relationship. So now the banquet is full, the banquet of love. Jesus says this is the kingdom of God. It is the place of love. It is the community of love where each person is precious, each person is important, each person is a child of God.

We can understand how important a parable like this is for the people of L'Arche, the people in Faith and Life communities, and for the community of Saint Martin. Our society wants people to be efficient, capable, and successful. This is the culture of competition, a culture that has been fostered by the media and that has become a way of life. We must do, we must succeed; but what happens to those who cannot succeed?

We see a society that accepts only those who are capable. God, however, is there, holding on to those who are deemed incapable, those who are considered a nuisance. God holds them and loves them.

## ⌒ *God has chosen the weak*

St. Paul had a deep sense of God's presence in the most vulnerable. He began by persecuting the disciples of Jesus, but then he met Jesus and was transformed. In this meeting, he discovered a unique relationship; he discovered that he was loved. Then he discovered that the weakest, the littlest, were the ones who accepted Jesus easily. This is why in Corinthians Paul says that God chose the weak and the foolish to shame those who want power, ideas, and knowledge. Paul goes on to say that God has chosen the most despised.

The challenge for us is that Jesus offers love, love that comes through relationship. The question to us is, Do I want to create an identity of power, or do I want to accept the relationship offered? Each one of us has a history, one of pain and one of joy, one of welcome and one of rejection. Maybe we are depressed and angry, or maybe we feel rejected by our parents because we have not been as welcomed as we would have wanted to be. My hope is that whoever we are, whatever our story, whatever difficulties in life we face because of sickness, rejection, or failure, or on the contrary, because of good health and success, that each one of us will be able to say: Don't worry. Jesus loves me as I am. In my fragility, in my vulnerability, in all the disappointments of my life, and in all the moments of joy in my life, Jesus loves me.

Right now, today, we can live and experience the love of God. This we can do by setting aside moments of silence, because God reveals himself essentially through silence, in moments of peace, and in the moments of inner quiet.

# ∽ *Whose fault is it?*

Many of us feel ashamed of our past and of our story. I am always touched when I listen to mothers who feel ashamed because they have a son or a daughter with a disability. They feel that they are being punished for their sins and their disabled children are the result of this curse. In the ninth chapter of the Gospel of John, we see Jesus and the disciples coming out of the temple. They meet a beggar who has been blind since birth. The immediate reaction of the disciples is to ask, "Whose fault is it that this man has been born blind? Is it because of his parents' sin or because he has sinned?"

In some cultures, there is a deep belief that if you have a son or a daughter with disabilities, it serves as evidence that you have committed a sin or that your parents committed a sin, or that someone has done something wrong. To have a child like this is considered a punishment. This is why parents frequently hide these children away: nobody must know that my child has a severe disability. They are hidden away in big institutions or within families or just abandoned on the street.

When the disciples ask Jesus about the beggar and the origin of his plight, Jesus tells them that there is no question of sin, no question of fault. He tells them that the man was born blind so that the work of God may be accomplished! What is this work of God? It is love, so that all may grow in love, so that the family may grow in love, so that the village may grow in love, and in the end, all may know their place in the family and in the Church.

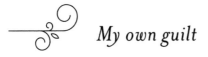 *My own guilt*

Many of us carry around guilt. We have not been the success that we wanted to be, or maybe we have hurt people. We may also have contracted a disease, or we might feel that we have not followed Jesus as we should have. We may feel guilty because we have difficulty relating with others, or because we desire power more than we do relationships. Each one of us carries around guilt. This guilt makes it difficult for us to say: Do not worry. Jesus loves me as I am.

Maybe this is easier for the little boy to say than it is for the adult. Yet Jesus is waiting to receive each one of us as we are, with our difficulties in relationships, with our fears, and with our need to prove ourselves. What is important is that we live an experience of God that will permit us to say: Jesus loves me as I am.

This, however, does not mean that everything is perfect. If I discover that Jesus loves me, I will want to grow in that love and tell others about it. When I live an experience of being loved by Jesus as I am, it does not mean that there is nothing else to do. It is simply the beginning of a journey.

 *Be open*

I call you to be open to an experience with Jesus, to spare a moment of silence that will help you to love yourself as you are. I have found that many of us have lost confidence in ourselves. Perhaps in our families, in our places of work, or in our schools, people have looked down on us. Maybe they have not admired us or they have rebuked or criticized us. Jesus wants to take away our distrust, or the lack of trust in ourselves, and to give to each one of us a little moment of inner peace.

We have to learn to contemplate one another, to look at one another with love. We must be able to offer a love that is neither possessive nor controlling. We receive and should offer a love that sees in the other person the presence of God, God who is deep within each one of us. We also need to take a moment of silence to be quiet—to be with Jesus and listen to the words: Do not worry. Jesus loves me as I am.

In this way, each one of us can start to give thanks for who we are. I can rejoice in who I am, with my broken history, my pain, my disability, my difficulties in relationships, and all that is part of my history. As we each discover that it is okay to be ourselves, we can start to grow in love and to become each day a little more like Jesus.

# CHAPTER 6

# Encountering the Other

Love your enemies.

Do good to those who hate you.

Bless those who curse you.

Pray for those who mistreat you.

(FROM LUKE 6)

What will cause me to change? What will transform me?

If I spend all my time criticizing others and don't see the positive in them, what will help me to change? This is the question.

I have spoken about the little boy who said, "Do not worry, mummy. Jesus loves me as I am."

Transformation comes with the recognition that I am loved, that I know I have gifts to share, and that I can do beautiful things. But mostly it is because I discover that I am loved.

## *When a child is not loved*

Many years ago, I visited a prison, and sometimes I would spend days there. Once, I stayed at the prison for an entire week. I had my cell just like the prisoners, and during the day I would give a retreat, but at other moments, prisoners would come to visit me. In one of the prison visits, I was asked to meet a man who had committed five murders. He had killed five women. As I approached his cell, I sensed vibrations of hate coming from him. It caused me a lot of pain. On entering his cell, I saw that he had no emotion on his face or in his eyes. There was just a sort of hotness coming out of his body.

I do not remember what we talked about, but I remember that as I left I began to reflect on what might have happened to him as a child. How does somebody end up like that? Why does someone close like a cement block, without emotions, openness, or kindness? What must he be living? It seemed that he must have suffered terribly during his childhood. Instead of being held with love, being treated and touched with tenderness, instead of having somebody tell him, "I love you," he might have been abandoned or perhaps been a victim or witnessed violence, or maybe he had been sexually abused. It might even have been a combination of these, or other unspeakable atrocities, that had been the story of his childhood.

Each of us has lived for months in the wombs of our mothers. When we are born, we are fragile and vulnerable and we have no defenses. We can easily be hurt. This is why there is need for a mother and a family to protect the child, and to help the child discover, "You are precious and loved. You are my son. You are my daughter. And I love you. You are unique and you are special." What happens if a child does not hear this? What happens if a child does not receive tenderness or if very quickly after the child is born his parents and family die? The child remains alone and frightened and is then obliged to build barriers. Some children have been brought up in a world where adults are enemies; these adults have hurt them and violated them in their vulnerability. For the man in prison, if no one ever treated him as a person during his life, how can he learn to treat other human beings well? He has to protect himself because he views others as enemies and not as people who may approach him with love.

 *I need you*

Jesus is the person who, when he was nailed naked to the cross, did not say he was frightened because he was naked, but said that he did not have to hide, even in his nakedness, because he knew that he was loved by God the Father. This is the movement from malediction to benediction. It is the same experience for the mothers and fathers of children with disabilities, who find, in the people of Saint

Martin, others who understand their pain. They are invited to come and be with people who will sing and dance with them, and where their child will find a place. Their child will no longer be excluded. It is nice to learn to say, "I need you. I need your love. I need your help. I cannot do it by myself." This is transformation: to discover an accepting community and then to discover Jesus.

In this growth and transformation, one of the important things I need to do is to put a finger on my fear, to understand that not only am I afraid of failure, and of not being loved, but in some ways, I am also governed by fear. It is important to acknowledge that these fears lead me into a world of lies and pretense, and it is important to touch those parts of my being where I am broken.

## ❧  *The need for quiet*

There is a need to experience the reality of silence, and in that silence to hear God saying, "You are precious in my eyes, and I love you." Each one of us needs to be refreshed, changed, and renewed. We can forget to pray, or we can fall into a pit of doubt and not know how to come out of it, but we can also take a moment of refreshment, renewal, and grasping a vision where it is okay to be vulnerable and it is okay to be ourselves. We can each find that place where we do not have to pretend that we are better than everyone else, or that our tribe is better than the next one, or that the color of our skin is better than another. Each of us needs to understand that we do not have to pretend anymore, that we are simply human beings, brothers and sisters, little children with our own gifts and weaknesses.

We all need a time of renewal. We need to refine the vision of Jesus, to refine the Gospel message so that it transforms us and gives us life. This time of renewal can be gentle and will be a moment when we touch difficult things within us, including our needs for power and superiority.

## Seeing people beyond their difficulties

Living in L'Arche has been very important for me. I had been someone who knew how to teach, and I knew how to give to others. Living in L'Arche, however, brought about a fundamental change in me. It brought me somewhere very different: to a reality of listening, understanding, and patience. I learned to take the time to understand people who are violent and angry and those who are anguished or depressed. I discovered many things that had to change in me. As this happened, little by little, Jesus helped me to see people beyond their difficulties and their handicaps—to see their humanity more deeply than all that was negative in them.

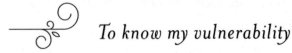

## *To know my vulnerability*

I wish to talk with you about Lucien, a thirty-four-year-old man with a deep psychosis. Lucien could neither walk nor speak. He couldn't eat by himself, and his body was catatonic. He lived in a terrible anguish of broken communion. When he felt a lot of inner pain, he would scream. There were times when he would go into this terrible anguish and he would scream, sometimes for two hours on end. We decided, with our doctors, that we would let him scream and not give him medication that would stop his screaming. He needed to express his pain. His screaming was difficult for us who lived with him, but to give him medication would have been to help us, which is not right.

What I discovered is that Lucien's screams awoke my own screams. His anguish awoke my own anguish.

Somewhere deep inside, I could not stand his screaming. Other people in that little home were able to welcome him better than I, during those moments.

Lucien's screams touched my nakedness. There is an inner poverty and anguish in each one of us, where our walls seem to collapse and we are left naked in front of others and ourselves. We are people of inner pain. I could feel it rising within me. There was hatred, or just a desire to get rid of Lucien. However, living in community, I knew that others were there; I did not have to run away or send Lucien away. Today, I can give thanks to Lucien because he revealed something about me that I needed to know—about my pain, about my own anguish, and about the violence that is within me. I needed to be able to speak about it without shame.

## The call to growth

This is my reality, and I must grow in it. I must accept it, walk through it, and speak about it. I need to ask Jesus to heal me so that I am not controlled by anguish, so that I do not hurt people, or imagine that I am superior in any way.

We have all lived experiences of rejection or failure, of being close to death, or where we have otherwise touched our creature-ness and come to the realization that we are not God. We are creatures. Some years ago, we did not exist, and in some years to come, we will not exist. Our souls and hearts can be in the heart of God, but our bodies will no longer exist and will become completely of the earth.

That is who I am—I am a creature. I am not God.

I am a broken man like all human beings, but I also know that Jesus loves me and that he is calling me to grow. This is the experience of being loved in my brokenness, and therein lies the incredible gentleness of our God. We all have to discover the point of our brokenness because that is precisely the place where we are the beloved.

Sometimes we hide behind the idea that we are better than others. We have to discover that none of us is better, that we are all children of God who have been called to grow, to become men and women of peace in our world, where there is still too much rejection for those who are fragile and vulnerable.

God has a dream, or at least a vision, a desire, to bring people together in love. There are two fundamental things that Jesus came to reveal to us. First, God is a lover. God loves. Second, this incredible, gentle, and tender God is in love with each one of us. Each person is precious to God, and together we are to build a community where we love one another.

## *We can heal one another*

In the community of Saint Martin it was discovered that there were many people in pain and misery and nobody knew about them. When these needs were made manifest, what happened? The dream of Saint Martin unfolded, and volunteers came forward. Extraordinarily, people came out of their world of business and family, and suddenly new energy was found among the people and they wanted to serve. People discovered that they could give life to others.

This is the extraordinary thing that happens when it becomes evident that others are suffering and crying out for relationship. Many people, who did not know about these needs, rise up. They say, "I can help!"

We can heal one another. It is not only about volunteers hearing of those who are in difficulty; it is also about the poor who permit people to rise with new energy and permit them to come out and discover that they can love. The reality is that the volunteers themselves are being healed as they assume responsibility to give life. The blessing you receive in your encounter with the poor is that you will be changed. As you meet the many needs of orphaned children who are also HIV/AIDS positive, young girls who have been abused, people with disabilities hidden in their homes, and young people who have entered into a world of delinquency, you are called forth to say, "How can I help?" Thus are born many volunteers who then assume responsibility not just for their family, or their church, but for something wider.

## ✑ꙶ *To become peacemakers*

If we are to become peacemakers, we have to touch the places within ourselves where there is that fear. What Martin Luther King Jr. did was not easy. There is a lot of pain in the history of the relationship between black and white people in the United States. Sometimes the police were brutal, and when there were marches, people were beaten up. One can work for nonviolence, but when you are nonviolent in front of violent people you will surely be beaten up. This is clear in history and in the life of Dr. King. People found freedom because others accepted being beaten up; they accepted pain, and even death. I am not saying that we all should seek to be beaten. What I am saying is that there should be growth toward unity—a growth toward greater love.

Oscar Romero, an archbishop in El Salvador, took up the cause of the poor and the marginalized. He dared to speak out against the military that was siding with the big landowners. He stood up for people who had no land and talked about Jesus in the Gospel, only to be assassinated while celebrating Mass. He was assassinated just as Martin Luther King Jr. and Roger Schultz of Taizé were—because there was goodness, love, truth, and light in them, which was unbearable for some people. To follow Jesus is to work for peace. However, there are some in the world who want chaos and war because they benefit by perpetuating war and terrorism.

To stand by the poor, to visit the sick, to clothe the naked, to visit parents whose children have been pushed aside, means that you may be laughed at. However, this follows the message of Jesus: that as you get close to the weak, you will be healed and become more human. When you live in a society full of competition, where you find yourself seeking only your own success, you may gain power and money, but you will end up losing what is most valuable in becoming human: to be in relationship, open to another person. This is the vision of Jesus and the work of peace: to discover that every person is unique, whatever their disabilities, whatever their tribe, country, culture, or religion.

# ⌒○⌒ *My heart of stone*

At the heart of the message of Jesus is his fundamental call to bring peace—that is, to destroy the walls that separate us and to ensure that we are no longer governed by fear that causes us to close up. Jesus has come to change my heart of stone into a heart of flesh—to open my heart.

A heart of stone is a heart that is closed because of fear. The gift of Jesus is to reveal how much we are loved and also to help each one of us become aware of those parts of our being where we are closed—to help us understand that we have hearts of stone. This is a long and painful journey that does not happen overnight. Changing from a heart of stone, a heart closed and hard, into a heart of flesh, open and gentle, happens slowly. The vision of Jesus—to love your enemies, to do good to those who hate you, to speak well of those who speak badly of you, and to pray for those who push you down and persecute you—sounds crazy. It seems as if it is not possible!

## Who is my enemy?

I would like you to ask yourself, Who is your enemy? Who is that person that you are afraid of? Who is that person you would be happy if they disappeared? Who is that person who has hurt you so much?

I remember a woman coming up to me during a retreat and saying, "I am beginning to discover that my husband is my enemy. He is happy when I do the cooking and look after the children, but he never listens to me, and neither does he ask me anything. He treats me as if I am stupid. All he wants is for me to do the things that make him comfortable. I am now beginning to see all the anger I have in me against him. I am beginning to see that he is my enemy, and yet Jesus is asking me to forgive him. I do not know how to forgive him, because I bear too much anger against him."

We all have enemies. They could be within our own families or in our community circle. There are people that we despise and who we want to get rid of. You may have a lot of anger and pain within you toward your father, if he is alcoholic, or maybe if you have been sexually abused. It is important to bring this anger and pain into our minds, into our hearts. We might know people that we cannot forgive, and we would like them to disappear and die. We need to bring all this up, to let it come gently and slowly, and then at a particular moment we will hear Jesus saying, "No longer love your enemies in a very general way, but love this person."

There are different categories of enemies. There are those who are very visible because they create turmoil within us, and then there are those that we do not realize are enemies because we have pushed them aside. We never talk to them. We do not want to know that they exist. For some people, these enemies are people with disabilities: they live their lives as if they do not exist. They are enemies that we just do not want to know about or we do not want to get too close to, because we have shut them out. To us, Jesus is saying, "Love."

You will naturally feel resistant to the word of Jesus and find yourself answer, "I cannot." You will be surprised at how Jesus will respond. He will say, "I understand your pain. I understand that you cannot love this person." To that wife he will say, "I understand that you cannot love your husband. He has hurt you too much. He has used you and abused you. I understand the anger that you have against him." Jesus understands; he does not condemn; he does not judge. He understands. But then he might say, "Do you want me to help you? Do you want me to show you the road to making peace? Can I help you?" You might not be ready. You might say, "No! I cannot love this person." Or, "I hate this or that person." My advice to you is, if you say no, you could add, "I'm not ready. Come back in a few months, because today I am not ready to love my enemy. I am not ready to love this person in my community, or my brother or my sister who has hurt me. I just cannot." And Jesus will say, "I understand, but do you want me to help you so that your heart of stone can become a heart of flesh?"

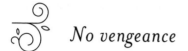 *No vengeance*

Hatred, or the refusal to love, can become like an inner sickness, like a cancer or gangrene. It can spread.

Our inability to love and to accept the other, to accept those who are different, to see behind the difficulties and the handicaps of the other, is a long journey, and it takes time and help. We need help to become people of peace. We need a community, and we need the grace of Jesus. So when Jesus asks, "Do you want me to help you?" let us open our hearts. Then Jesus will show us, little by little, how we can grow to a place of understanding and compassion.

Forgiveness is not just a big spiritual emotion. It can be that, but it also needs the human element of understanding. We come to understand the pain of the other, and where that person is coming from. It is like the man I mentioned in prison who had killed five women. Of course he should be in prison; of course he should be hidden away; but we must also try to understand and see what can be done to help him move from the violence he carries within, to discover who he is as a human being.

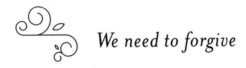

## We need to forgive

The mystery of Jesus is a mystery of forgiveness. We say in the prayer of Jesus, "Forgive us." All of us need to be forgiven, and we need to forgive. It is obvious that I have hurt people both intentionally and unintentionally. I have also failed to do things well, seeking my own power. I need to ask for forgiveness. Many of us need to ask for forgiveness from the poor because we have despised them or pushed them out of sight. We must kneel down and ask for their forgiveness. The history of humanity can only come to unity if we ask for forgiveness, one from the other. Forgiveness is not just the recognition that I am broken; it is also the recognition that I have broken others and that I have hurt them and helped prevent them from opening to the grace of God. The great mystery of Jesus is that he came to forgive, not just all that is broken in me, but all that I have broken in others. This is forgiveness.

Our God is a God of tenderness and forgiveness. Regardless of what we have done or not done in the past or present, let us stand up and start on the path of forgiving those who have hurt us, and seeking forgiveness from those we have hurt. In this way we will become a people who love one another, the barriers will begin to fall, and we will see in one another the presence of Jesus—the beauty of each person revealing the beauty of God.

Jesus shares a message that is surprising. It is easy to love people who love you. It is easy to lend to somebody who lends to you, or to someone who you know will pay you back. But the vision of Jesus is entirely new. It is about transformation, people standing up, rising up, and saying, "I can help, I can do something." Being exposed to pain brings up a new strength, vision, and responsibility toward the poor and the weak. This vision calls the rich out of their richness and into a community, a fraternity, a new love. It is taking the word of Jesus, "Love your enemies," and calling forth the desire to work for a world of peace.

# CHAPTER 7

# The Washing of the Feet

Fully aware that the Father had put everything into his power and that he had come from God and was returning to God, he rose from supper and took off his outer garments.

He took a towel and tied it around his waist.

Then he poured water into a basin and began to wash the disciples' feet and dry them with the towel around his waist.

So when he had washed their feet he said to them, "Do you realize what I have done for you? You call me 'teacher' and 'master,' and rightly so, for indeed I am.

If I, therefore, the master and teacher, have washed your feet, you ought to wash one another's feet.

I have given you a model to follow, so that as I have done for you, you should also do."

(FROM JOHN 13)

They were all seated, sharing a meal, when Jesus suddenly stood up and took off his clothes. He took off his garments, and you can almost imagine the apostles looking at one another asking, "What is he doing?"

Jesus was, as usual, wearing a long robe, under which he had a sort of shirtlike garment called a tunic that normally went down to the knees. Jesus took off this top robe, poured water into a basin, and then began to wash the feet of his disciples. They could not understand what was happening—Jesus taking off his clothes in the middle of a meal!

We begin to discover who Jesus is. Jesus loves us utterly; he knows that we are afraid of being loved, afraid of love, and that we are afraid of God. The entire message of Jesus is to tell us: "Do not be afraid." Jesus knew that the next day he would be killed, assassinated like Martin Luther King Jr., Oscar Romero, Mahatma Gandhi, Roger Schultz, and others. Humanity has had a history of killing men and women who speak the truth, call people to love, and proclaim that love is more important than power. They have all been killed. We all know that the history of humanity is frequently a history of dictators who impose power and crush people. Jesus came to show humanity something different. He came to call people forth: to help them stand up and to create community, places where we can love one another. This is the work of our extraordinarily humble and vulnerable Jesus.

When you love someone deeply, you want to be close to them. If that person says, "No, I do not want to have any contact with you," your heart will surely be wounded. We have all had the experience of loving someone who turned away from us. This is what happens with Jesus: he loves us, wants to liberate us, wants to help us grow and to continue his mission of love in this world. Instead, we turn away.

# Vocation

We know that this world is a painful place. Jesus came into the world to bring peace. After his death, he asked us to follow him so that you and I would be peacemakers. We all have a vocation.

Sometimes I'm a bit concerned when we talk of vocations, making reference only to the priesthood or religious life for sisters. I believe in the priesthood and I believe in religious life, but I also believe in the vocation of people with disabilities. I believe in the vocation of hearts filled with love of people like Maimuna and Dorothy and many others. We each have a vocation. We are all called by God to grow in love and be a sign of tenderness in the world. Our vulnerable Jesus is calling us to grow in love.

During the special meal where Jesus takes off his clothes and kneels to wash the feet of his disciples, Peter reacts and asks him, "What? You, wash my feet?", Jesus tells him, "You cannot understand this now, but later you will." Then Peter proclaims, "No, you shall never wash my feet!" Peter is very human. Before the Resurrection and Pentecost, he viewed humanity like a social pyramid, with those having power, privileges, and riches at the top, and the large number of everyone else at the bottom. More or less, isn't this the vision we all have of society? At the top are the powerful ones, and at the bottom are the useless ones, those who have little value. This is the entrenched vision that Jesus came to change. Society is not a pyramid but a body, and in that body each part is important. There are no parts that are the best or better than others. No! We are all together in that one body, each of us having our particular vocation. Sisters who are religious are not better than women who are married. Priests are not better than men who are married, and neither of them is better than people with disabilities. We are all together in a body, which is the body of Christ, and this is the Church where each person is important. We all have a vocation to love Jesus.

Peter did not understand. Jesus is the Messiah, the Son of God. I should wash his feet, not he wash mine! In Peter's culture, someone who knelt at the feet of another and washed their feet was considered a slave. So Peter said, "No, you can't wash my feet!" Do you know what Jesus said in response to Peter's protest? He said something extraordinary: "If you do not let me wash your feet, you can have no more part with me; you can no longer be my friend. If I cannot wash your feet, there is the door and you can leave."

## Who is God?

Jesus wants to reveal to us who God is. God is not a God of power who judges, hurts, shouts, or gives laws and directives. Rather, God is the one who created heaven and earth—the God of love, of tenderness, and the Word who became flesh. God is the little child of the woman Mary. The vision of Jesus is to announce the Good News to the poor, free the captives, give sight to the blind, and liberate all people who have been oppressed.

Jesus's vision is to make known to those who have been rejected and are poor, "I love you. You are loved by my Father." Jesus is no longer dealing with a social pyramid but with a body where each person has a place, every man and woman and every person with a disability. "My commandment is that you love one another as I love you, and they will know that you are my disciples by the love you have one for another and by the respect you have one for another." So, when Jesus says to Peter, "I am not going to oblige you: if you do not want to have your feet washed, you can go," Peter does not understand. He does not realize that what Jesus has said to him, he has said out of a generous heart. Do we understand Jesus?

## Go and do likewise

Once Jesus finished washing the feet of the disciples and put his clothes back on, he sat down and said: "Do you understand what I have done? You called me

Lord and Master, and so I am. If I have washed your feet, you must wash each other's feet. I have done this as an example for you."

This is the only place in the Gospel where Jesus says, "I have done this as an example. What I have done to you, you must do one to another." Then he said, "Amen, amen, I say to you. The servant is not more important than the master. The one who is sent is not more important than the one who sends. If I have done this for you, you must do this one to another. Know this: if you do it, your action will become a benediction for you."

Jesus loves us so much that he kneels in front of us so that we may begin to trust ourselves. As Jesus washes our feet, he is saying, "I trust you and I love you. You are important to me." Jesus kneeling in front of each one is saying, "You are precious. You are important, and I want you to trust yourself because you can do beautiful things for the kingdom. You can give life; you can bring peace. I want you to discover how important you are, and all I am asking is that you believe in yourself because you are a beloved child of God."

This is the humility of Jesus: he kneels at our feet! We cannot understand this. All of us know that if Jesus appeared and started kneeling at our feet and washing them, we would be embarrassed and not know what to do. This is Jesus. We have to discover who he is, who God is, and how much he loves us.

We need to help each person discover how important he or she is. Jesus is not washing our feet because our feet are dirty. It is a sign that he loves us and that each one of us is called to grow. This is Jesus performing a sacred act, and he's asking us to do this one to another: to love and to forgive one another. He calls us to work to build the body of Christ. He calls us to build a body that works together in love and friendship, rather than a pyramid where we seek more power than good. The washing of feet is a symbol that says, "I want to be at your service. I am not here to gain power or riches; I am here simply to serve you. I am here to serve so that you may grow and discover how beautiful you are."

CHAPTER 8

# *Come Out*

Martha and Mary sent word to Jesus, "Lord, the one you love is sick."

When he heard this, Jesus said, "This sickness will not end in death."

When Mary reached the place where Jesus was, she fell at his feet and said, "Lord, if you had been here, my brother would not have died."

When Jesus saw her weeping, he was deeply moved in spirit and troubled.

"Where have you laid him?" he asked.

"Come and see, Lord," they replied.

Jesus wept.

Then the Jews said, "See how he loved him!"

Jesus, once more deeply moved, came to the tomb.

It was a cave with a stone laid across the entrance.

"Take away the stone," he said.

So they took away the stone.

Jesus called in a loud voice, "Lazarus, come out!"

The dead man came out.

Jesus said to them, "Take off the grave clothes and let him go."

(FROM JOHN 11)

This Gospel reading begins with the two sisters sending a message to Jesus about their brother. The message says this: "The one you love is sick." I have always found this amazing.

The sisters do not say, "My brother is sick." They do not say, "Lazarus is sick." They just say, "The one you love is sick."

There are only two people in the Gospels who are referred to as "the one who is loved": Lazarus and John. In this passage, it is emphasized that Jesus loved Mary, Martha, and Lazarus, and Jesus also says "my friend Lazarus." Yet Lazarus does not speak. It is difficult to know who he is. Who is this Lazarus? Who is this man who does not speak and who Jesus follows?

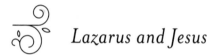 ## *Lazarus and Jesus*

In the Gospel of Luke, Jesus visits the house of Martha and Mary, and it is called "the house of Martha." In Jewish culture, we would normally talk about the house of Lazarus—but Lazarus is not mentioned. This seems strange because it is not according to Jewish custom. My conclusion is that Lazarus has a severe disability, which is why he seems in some ways absent. What is strange in the Catholic Church today is that there is a feast day for Mary, a feast day for Martha, but no feast day for Lazarus. We almost seem to forget people with disabilities. Lazarus is one of only two people in the Gospels about whom it is said that Jesus loved, yet there is no feast day for him.

As I said, the story begins with the two sisters sending a message to Jesus: "The one you love is sick." I like to interpret these words as: The one you came and fed, the one you gave a bath to, the one you played with, the one you love, is sick. Jesus, however, does not come straightaway. He waits. During this waiting period Lazarus dies. It is about four days later that Jesus arrives in Bethany. To everybody else Jesus says, "Follow me," but here Jesus is following Lazarus. Jesus arrives in Bethany, and the sisters, Martha and Mary, are weeping. Lazarus has already been buried.

When he reaches the tomb, Jesus stands and weeps. I think Jesus weeps over the world. Our world does not want the message of love. Our world always wants a message of power and success. Jesus comes to offer something else.

In that place near Bethany, Jesus wept. The two sisters are in pain, and Jesus arrives late. Martha hears that Jesus is there, rushes to him, and throws herself at his feet and says, "Lord, if you had been here, my brother would not have died." It is a slight reproach: Why did you wait? Why didn't you come earlier? If you had been here, my brother would not have died. Jesus just looks at her and says, "Your brother will rise again." "Yes," Martha says, "I know he will rise at the last moment. He is dead now, but I know that whatever you ask of God, he will hear you."

"He who believes in me will never die," says Jesus. "I know you are Christ, the Son of the living God," Martha replies.

Martha is a beautiful woman, filled with faith, and she rushes back into the house and whispers to Mary, "The Lord is here and is calling you." Mary, the younger sister, is weeping because she loved Lazarus deeply, like a mother who loves her child with a severe disability. She rushes down to Jesus. Jesus is still there at the entrance of the village of Bethany, and Mary says, "Lord, if you had been here, my brother would not have died." At this point, there is a moving moment when it is recorded that when Jesus saw Mary weeping at his feet, he too was moved. "Where have you put him?" Jesus asks. "Come and see," replies Mary. Jesus weeps. Something happens within Jesus. I dare say that something breaks within him and he is in anguish.

 ## Come out

Here we discover that Jesus is profoundly human, deeply loving. We see Jesus weeping. They have brought him to the tomb where Lazarus is buried, and Jesus is deeply moved. He says, "Take away the stone." Martha, a well-organized woman, says to Jesus, "But he smells! He has been dead for four days." Martha prefers to tell Jesus what to do instead of listening. Jesus looks at her and says, "Didn't I tell you that if you believe, you will see the glory of God?" That is, if you trust. These words are for us—if you trust, you will see the glory of God. The Gospel of John says that the glory of God is that you bear fruits and realize that what you are doing for love comes from God, and that you have become his instrument.

Then Jesus prays: "Father, I know that you will always accept my prayer, and now I pray so that they may believe." And Jesus cries out: "Lazarus, come out!"

Maybe today Jesus is thinking about each of our names and he is saying to each of us: "Come out! Stand up and do not be afraid. Come out from the tomb. Stand up and believe." Maybe the great sufferance of God is not just that we don't believe in Jesus, but also that we don't believe in ourselves. This may be the result of past humiliations, or because we have been told that we are not good enough. We do not realize that each one of us is sick like Lazarus: "the one you love is sick." Maybe Lazarus represents each of us with our disability. Jesus says, "Untie him," and gives Lazarus back to the two sisters. I love to imagine this scene where Mary is amazed to see her brother coming back from the dead. She does not know whether to throw herself into Lazarus's arms, or throw herself into the arms of Jesus.

## *I will put my spirit within you*

This resurrection reminds us of the prophet Ezekiel, who tells us about that great vision of a valley of death: "I will open your graves, O my people, and I will put my spirit within you and you shall live."

This prophecy took place about three centuries before what happened at Lazarus's tomb in Bethany. We can see the relationship between Ezekiel's vision, the bringing back of Lazarus from the dead, and the bringing to life of all that is dead within us. Our fears, hatred, and incapacities to love and forgive are the graves in which we are enclosed. "Behold, I will open your grave and raise you, O my people. And you shall know I am the Lord." Everyone loved by Jesus is called from the grave to stand and receive a mission of love. Jesus calls to those parts of us that are dead, those parts of us that are controlled by fear of failure or not being loved. All those fears that prevent us from entering into the vision of Jesus: a Church where the weakest people transform us by their presence. This is how it began in Saint Martin when it became known that there were people with disabilities hidden away.

This is our resurrection. Jesus calls us from the tomb to give us his spirit, a spirit of love, wisdom, and community, for loving one another. This is the resurrection of Lazarus—this wounded, fragile man who did not speak, who had a handicap but was loved. For his family, Martha and Mary, it was all very moving, not only because their brother had come back to life, but we discover as we read the Gospel that when people there saw Lazarus coming from the tomb, many began to believe in Jesus and trust in him. To believe is not just something in the head, but it involves a trust that says: I trust that Jesus loves me and is calling me to grow and be part of community.

## To give my all

One week after the resurrection of Lazarus, there was a little reunion or celebration, and Jesus came. They all had a meal together. Martha was serving and Mary, whose heart was filled with love for Jesus, found a bottle containing precious and expensive ointment. She took the ointment and poured it on the feet of Jesus, her tears mingling with it, and then wiped his feet with her hair. The room where they were eating was filled with its perfume. A few days earlier, Martha had said that the body of Lazarus smelled because he was dead, and now the room was filled with the perfume of love, the perfume of resurrection. Mary loved Jesus so much that she wanted to give him her all. She wanted to give her life to Jesus. This is what Jesus is asking each one of us: to give our lives wherever we are because Jesus has given his life for us.

The disciples did not understand the relationship between Mary and Jesus. There was a sort of intimacy between them, a collision of love, which they didn't understand. This is why Judas begins to complain, saying, "She should not have wasted all that costly ointment on the feet of Jesus! We should have sold it and given the money to the poor." Sometimes there can be jealousy among men because women can have a deeper relationship with Jesus. The disciples think that they are the ones who deserve to have everything, so they criticize the woman.

Jesus must have been deeply touched because he knew he would soon be dead and here was Mary pouring what she considered the most precious thing to her onto his feet. Jesus does not accept the criticism, and he says, "This woman has done a beautiful thing, and when the Gospel is written, what she has done here will be announced to the whole world." Jesus defended Mary. He said, "I am with you only for a short time, and afterward the poor will always be here." There seems to be a double meaning: it is right, it is good, and it is for the glory of God that this woman, Mary, has given this precious ointment to Jesus and put it on his feet. I would even say she "wasted" it on him, because to love someone is to "waste" our time and to give our gifts. Mary poured what was most precious on his feet just to say, "I love you." Then Jesus said, "The poor you will always have, but not me," by which I think he meant: From now on, I will be manifested in the poor, the weak, and the broken. I will die crucified and rejected, and I will return to the Father. With the Father I will send the Spirit, and you will come out from your grave and discover that I am present in the poorest, the weakest, the broken, the lost, and in the people with disabilities who have been rejected.

Jesus sends out his disciples so that they may discover his presence in all those who are broken, lost, and have no hope. It is here that we begin to discover that as we go to the poor and the broken, they change our lives and make us become more human. And in becoming more human and loving, we become better disciples of Jesus.

# About Jean Vanier, L'Arche, and Faith and Light

Jean Vanier is a humanist, philosopher, theologian, and man of letters who is first and foremost described by his companions as a man with heart and compassion. A passionate advocate for humanity and truth, he was awarded the Templeton Prize in 2015. Past recipients include Archbishop Desmond Tutu, H.H. the Dalai Lama, and Brother Roger Schultz.

The first L'Arche Community was started in 1964 in Trosly-Breuil, a village in the north of Paris, France, when Jean Vanier invited two people with intellectual disabilities to live with him in a small house. This house he named L'Arche, which is French for "The Ark," a name that has been adopted by all the communities around the world that have been founded on similar principles, where assistants live the same experience of the encounter that Jean first did. Today, L'Arche is made up of 151 communities spread over five continents. There are more than five thousand members in all.

Parallel to L'Arche Communities, Jean Vanier cofounded Faith and Light with Marie-Hélène Mathieu, "communities of encounter" that are woven around people, adults or children, living together with intellectual disabilities. These people, accompanied by their families and friends, are invited to participate in monthly meetings, during which time they share friendship, prayer, and celebration. Faith and Light has nearly one thousand five hundred such communities in eighty one countries on five continents.